BUILT
by Angels

BUILT
by Angels

THE STORY OF THE OLD-NEW SYNAGOGUE

MARK PODWAL

Harcourt Children's Books   Houghton Mifflin Harcourt

New York 2009

Requests for permission to make copies of any part of the work should be submitted online
at www.harcourt.com/contact or mailed to the following address:
Permissions Department, Houghton Mifflin Harcourt Publishing Company,
6277 Sea Harbor Drive, Orlando, Florida 32887-6777.

Harcourt Children's Books is an imprint of
Houghton Mifflin Harcourt Publishing Company.

www.hmhbooks.com

Library of Congress Cataloging-in-Publication Data
Podwal, Mark H., 1945–
Built by angels: the story of the old-new synagogue/Mark Podwal.
p. cm.
1. Synagogues—Czech Republic—Prague—Juvenile fiction.
2. Jews—Czech Republic—Prague—Juvenile fiction. I. Title.
BM653.P63 2009
296.4'6—dc22   2007052091
ISBN 978-0-15-206678-9

First edition
A C E G H F D B

Printed in Singapore

The illustrations in this book were done in acrylic, gouache,
and colored pencil on Cason paper.
The display type was created by Monica Dengo.
The text type was set in Requiem Fine and Captain Kidd Lowercase.
Color separations by Colourscan Co. Pte. Ltd., Singapore
Printed and bound by Tien Wah Press, Singapore
Production supervision by Pascha Gerlinger
Jacket designed by Michele Wetherbee
Interior designed by Lydia D'moch and Michele Wetherbee

For my friends in Prague,

whose synagogue was built by angels

Prayer is the way people talk to God.
Though a prayer can be said anywhere,
the synagogue is where Jewish people
come together to pray.
Where the first synagogue was
has long ago been forgotten,
but there is a synagogue,
older than any other,
in which Jews still pray.
A synagogue with as many
stories as stones.

Square stones, round stones,

stone doors, stone floors,

stones carved like leaves,

others like grapes,

all brought by angels, they say,

to the beautiful city of Prague,

where, stone by stone,

the angels built a synagogue.

A thousand years later,
when Jews came to Prague,
they saw many majestic churches,
but found no special place
for Jews to pray.

And then an angel,

disguised as a beggar,

led the Jews to a barren hill

and told them to dig.

There they uncovered the synagogue

the angels had built.

Although old, it mysteriously looked new.

As the beggar departed,

he made it known that

all the synagogue stones

were from the Temple in Jerusalem,

which ancient enemies had destroyed.

Someday every stone

would have to be returned.

Until then, warned the beggar,

if a single stone was moved or changed in any way,

the whole synagogue

would crumble and collapse.

Small stones, large stones,
stone seats, stone steps,
a stone carved like a star,
others painted with words,
all in the synagogue
the people named
Old-New.

Under the star-shaped stone,

men and women were wed.

Beside the stones painted with words,

children learned to read.

The melodies of the prayers

were so beautiful,

even the birds sang them.

For two days each spring,
the synagogue walls would be adorned
with countless leaves,
recalling how the desert blossomed
when the Ten Commandments
were read aloud by God.

And on the holiest of days,

when the synagogue

was so crowded with people

that no one could force a finger between them,

the stones made space for everyone

to bow down in prayer.

As long as anyone can remember,
a piece of Passover matzoh, the *afikomen,*
hung in the synagogue all year round.
It was said to have special powers
to protect against harm.
Again and again, miracles
saved the synagogue from ruin.
Whenever flames threatened,
white doves would circle its tiled roof.
And the beating of their wings
blew out the blaze.

In the hours after midnight,
few were willing to pass
near the synagogue,
for it was believed
ghosts gathered there to pray
in the moonlight.
Before entering in the morning,
worshippers would bang
on the synagogue door
to remind the ghosts
it was time to leave.

Hundreds of years ago,
from a lump of clay,
the Great Rabbi Loew
molded a golem,
a man of colossal strength,
to clean the synagogue's windows
and sweep its stone floors.

And still today,

locked in the dusty attic,

buried beneath cobwebs and holy books,

rests the golem who must not be disturbed,

lest it go wild

and hurl houses into the clouds,

as it once did, causing Rabbi Loew

to turn it back into clay.

So beloved was the rabbi,
since the day he died,
seat number one, his chair
by the synagogue's eastern wall,
has remained empty.

Across a narrow lane,

on the tower of the Jewish Town Hall,

backward round and round,

move the hands of the Hebrew clock.

As the hours, days, and years pass,

time has erased almost everything nearby.

Fashionable shops replaced
sagging houses.
Winding alleyways were widened
into boulevards.
And yet the Old-New Synagogue remains.
It welcomes all who come to pray.

Heavy stones, light stones,
stone pillars, stone walls,
stones carved like branches,
others like roots—
and as the angel decreed,
not one moved or changed in any way.
Stone by stone,
they echo the prayer
"Next year in Jerusalem!"
And wait to return.

Author's Note

Prague's Altneuschul, or Old-New Synagogue, is the oldest surviving synagogue in Europe. A place of haunting charm and mystery, the synagogue has withstood wars and pogroms, floods and fires, and an urban-clearing project at the end of the nineteenth century that destroyed most of the ancient Jewish Quarter. Legend says the Altneuschul was built by angels. History attributes its construction in 1270 to stonemasons working nearby on St. Agnes Convent. Initially called the New Synagogue, it later became known as the Old-New Synagogue (*Altneuschul* in German) after newer synagogues were established in the ghetto. Some say the name derives from the legend that its stones are from the destroyed Temple in Jerusalem, stones loaned "on condition" (*al-tenai* in Hebrew) that they be returned when the Temple is restored.

A treasure of early Gothic architecture, the synagogue's ceiling has an odd fifth rib believed to be added so that Jews would not have to pray beneath crosses formed by the intersecting ribs of a Gothic vault. Symbolizing the twelve tribes of Israel are twelve high windows. Each is narrow on the inside and wide on the outside so that the light of the synagogue would shine out to the world.

A custom peculiar to the Old-New Synagogue is that Psalm 92 is recited twice at Friday-evening services. Legend says that Rabbi Loew turned the golem back to clay every Friday before sunset since it, too, had to rest on the Sabbath. Yet once, the rabbi forgot to do so and the golem went berserk, destroying everything in its path. When he learned what was happening, Rabbi Loew interrupted the congregation's singing of Psalm 92, rushed to turn the golem back to clay, and then started the psalm again. To this day, Psalm 92 is always sung twice.

For centuries the walls of the Altneuschul were never to be whitened so that the bloodstains of those murdered there during a pogrom would not be concealed. Today, after many restorations, the marks on the synagogue's walls are Hebrew letters. Having endured through the ages, the Altneuschul continues not only as a place of worship but also as a testament to the perseverance of the Jewish people.

—MARK PODWAL

Bibliography

Lion, Jindřich. *The Prague Ghetto.* Translated by Jean Layton. London: Spring Books, n.d.

Pařik, Arno. *Prague Synagogues.* Prague: The Jewish Museum in Prague, 2000.

Ripellino, Angelo Maria. *Magic Prague.* Edited by Michael Henry Heim. Translated by David Newton Marinelli. Berkeley: University of California Press, 1994.

Trachtenberg, Joshua. *Jewish Magic and Superstition: A Study in Folk Religion.* New York: Berhman's Jewish Book House, 1939.